Transportation

Around the World

by Ellen Lawrence

Ruby Tuesday Books

Published in 2026 by Ruby Tuesday Books Ltd.

Copyright © 2026 Ruby Tuesday Books Ltd.

All rights reserved. No part of this publication may be reproduced in whole or in part, stored in any retrieval system, or transmitted in any form or by any means, electronic, mechanical, photocopying, recording, or otherwise, without written permission from the publisher.

Editor: Mark J. Sachner
Designers: Emma Randall & Tammy West
Production: John Lingham

Photo credits:
Lola Akinmade: 10; Alamy: 11 (ton koene), 20 (Andrew Aitchison), 21 (chrisstockphoto); FLPA: 12; Nature Picture Library: 14–15 (Bryan & Cherry Alexander/Orsolya Haarberg); Simon Phelps: 18–19; Public Domain: 16R; Shutterstock: Cover (Yongyut Kumsri), 4T (Alexandros Michailidis), 4B (Stefano Ember), 5 (Julia Agin/Rocky Siahaija), 6 (oneinchpunch), 7 (Muskoka Stock Photos), 8 (Perfect Lazybones), 9 (Nowak Lukasz), 13 (Yongyut Kumsri), 16L (cyo bo), 17 (Sk Hasan Ali).

Library of Congress Control Number: 2024948741

Hardback ISBN 978-1-78856-552-3
Paperback ISBN 978-1-78856-553-0
ePub ISBN 978-1-78856-554-7

Published in Minneapolis, MN
Printed in the United States

www.rubytuesdaybooks.com

The picture on the front cover of this book shows people in Greenland traveling by dog sled. Turn to page 13 to find out more about this type of transportation.

CONTENTS

We're All on the Move!... 4

Safe Yellow School Buses 6

A Rickshaw School Bus 8

Paddling to School 10

Animal Transportation..12

Follow the Reindeer!..14

Train Travel...16

Flying Ambulances..18

People Power..20

Welcome to My World 22

Glossary 23

Index 24

Words shown in bold in the text are explained in the glossary.

All the places in this book are shown on the map on page 22.

We're All on the Move!

All around the world, people are on the move.

We travel by car, van, bus, bike, and even reindeer!

In Guatemala, many people travel by bus. This bus was once a yellow school bus in the United States. Now it's been repainted and carries people from village to village.

Riding reindeer in Mongolia

It's all aboard in Indonesia!

Safe Yellow School Buses

Each morning, millions of children in the United States and Canada climb aboard a yellow school bus.

The bright yellow color was chosen to help keep children safe.

This color can be seen at dawn and in the late afternoon, when there's not much light.

Yellow school buses can also easily be seen in rainy, snowy, and foggy weather.

All school buses are the same shade of yellow. It's called National School Bus Glossy Yellow.

A Rickshaw School Bus

In India, some children travel to school in **rickshaws**.

Some of these small carriages are powered by an engine, a little like a motorbike.

The driver rides in the front.

Other rickshaws are pulled by a driver on foot or on a bicycle.

An engine-powered rickshaw

Some of the rickshaw school buses look a little like cages. Each one holds up to 10 children. The passengers' backpacks ride on the roof.

A driver-powered rickshaw

For many kids, the journey to school can take two hours!

Paddling to School

On a **lagoon** near Lagos, in Nigeria, school children paddle to school in small canoes.

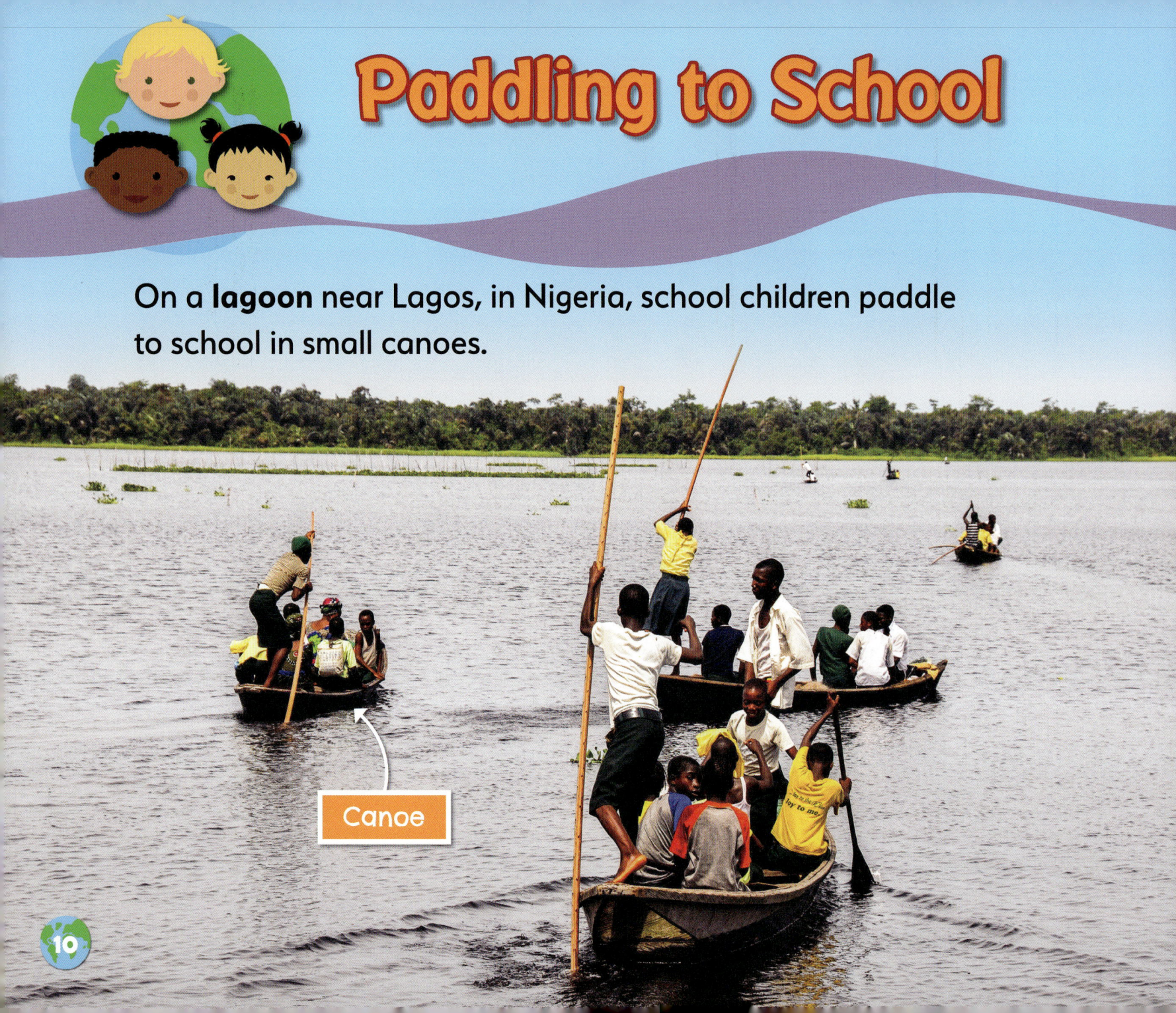

Canoe

The children live in fishing villages on one side of the lagoon.

Their school is on the other side of the lagoon.

The older kids paddle the canoes, while their younger friends enjoy the ride to school.

The children travel to school in the canoes that their fathers use for fishing. The men fish during the night. When they return from fishing early each morning, the kids head off to school.

A fisherman on the lagoon

Animal Transportation

People have traveled by horse and donkey power for about 5,000 years.

A donkey cart in Botswana

A horse and cart in Tibet

Horses and donkeys were once wild animals.

Over time, our **ancestors** tamed and trained them.

A sled dog team

In Greenland, Inuit people have traveled by dog sled for thousands of years. Each powerful dog in a team can pull one and a half times its own weight over snow and ice.

Follow the Reindeer!

In Norway, Sami reindeer **herders** live alongside their animals.

The large herds of reindeer move from place to place to find food.

The herders use snowmobiles to ride with their herds.

Reindeer herder

A tired baby reindeer

Train Travel

All around the world, people travel by train.

In China, people get to ride on the fastest train in the world.

The **maglev train** in the city of Shanghai reaches a top speed of 268 miles per hour (431 km/h).

Maglev train in Shanghai, China

A screen inside the train shows the speed.

This train in Bangladesh is crowded with people traveling to see their families on a holiday.

Flying Ambulances

In the **outback** of Australia, many people live hundreds of miles from a doctor or hospital.

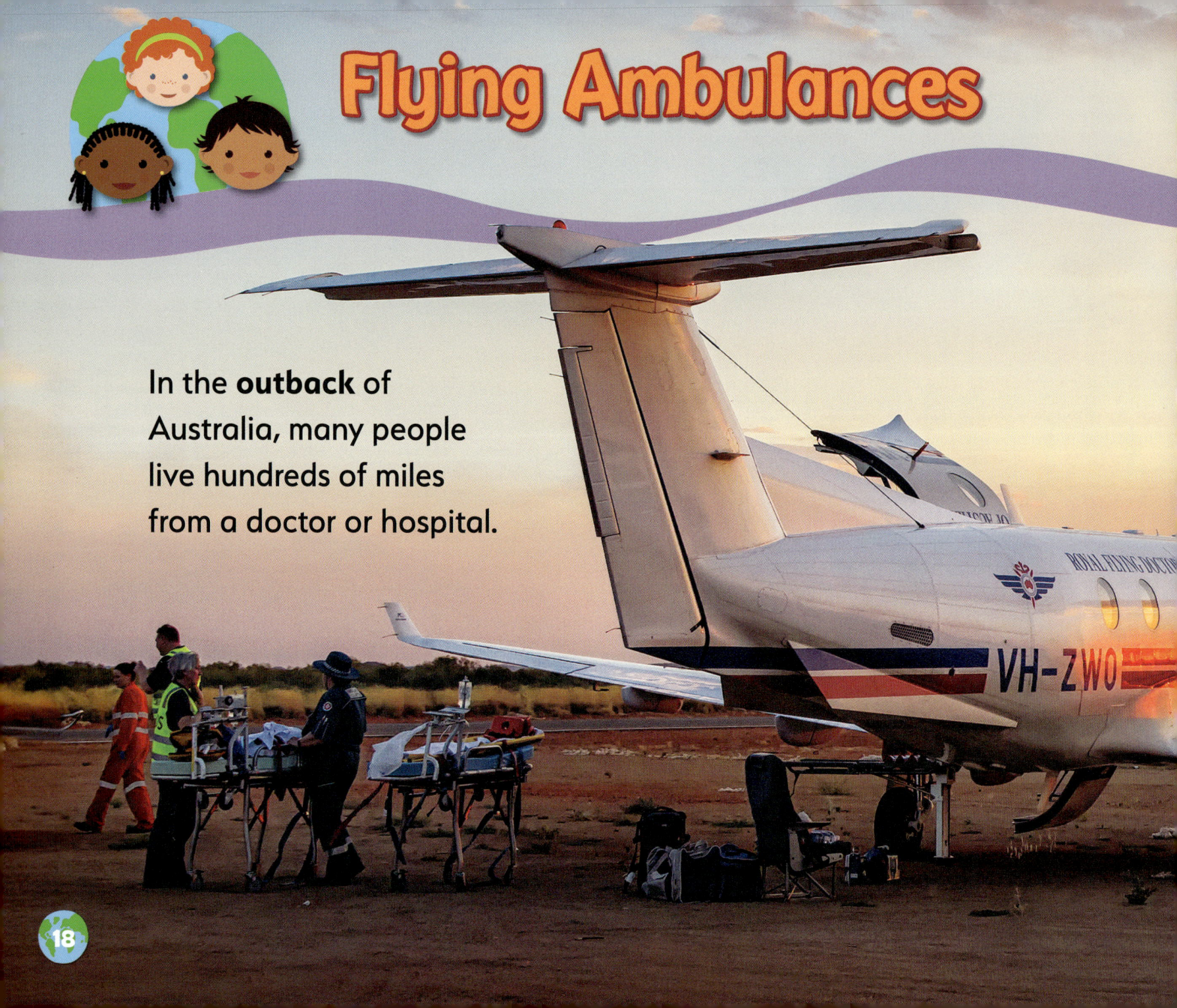

When people need help, doctors come to them by plane.

Sometimes the plane acts like a flying ambulance and carries a patient to the nearest hospital.

A flying doctor might even operate on a patient inside the plane!

The flying doctors' planes often have to land on rocky, rough ground where there is no airstrip, or runway. The people waiting for the doctor use their car headlights to show the plane where to land.

A flying doctors' plane

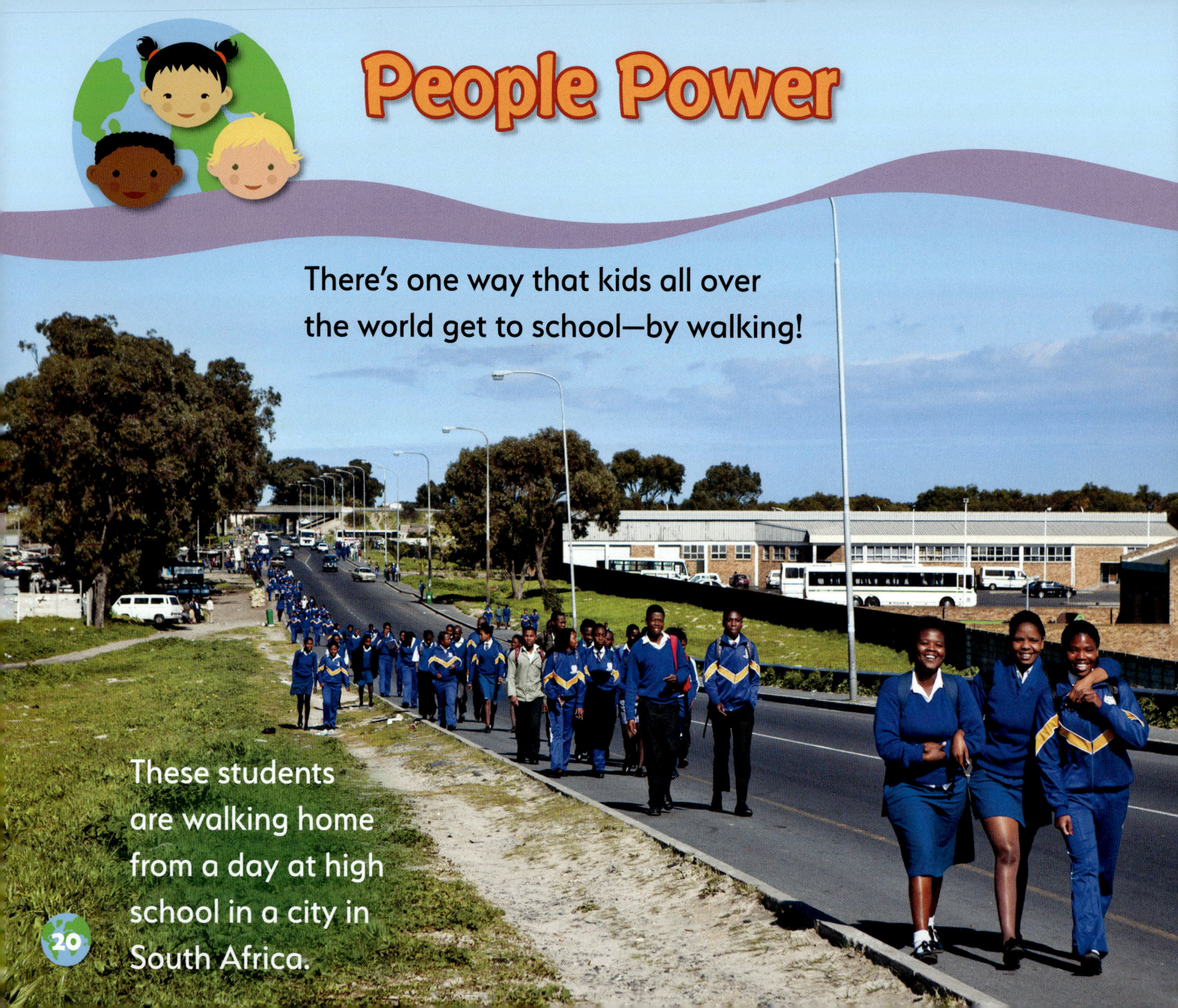

People Power

There's one way that kids all over the world get to school—by walking!

These students are walking home from a day at high school in a city in South Africa.

In the United Kingdom, some children travel to school in a walking bus. Children and adults walk around town collecting kids from each street. Walking buses are great exercise and reduce **pollution** from cars.

A walking bus

Welcome to My World

Greenland
Page 13

United Kingdom
Page 21

Belgium
Page 4

Norway
Pages 14–15

Tibet, China
Page 12

Mongolia
Page 5

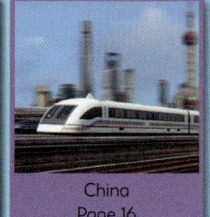
China
Page 16

North America

Europe

Asia

Africa

South America

Australia

United States and
Canada Pages 6–7

Guatemala
Page 4

Nigeria
Pages 10–11

Botswana
Page 12

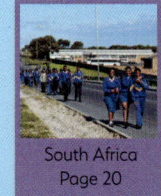
South Africa
Page 20

India
Pages 8–9

Bangladesh
Page 17

Indonesia
Page 5

Australia
Pages 18–19

GLOSSARY

ancestor
A relative who lived a long time ago. For example, your great-grandparents and great-great-grandparents are your ancestors.

herder
A person who spends their life caring for animals and moving, or herding, them from place to place so that the animals have enough to eat.

lagoon
A shallow lake or pool of saltwater. It is connected to the ocean but is separated from the open sea by a coral reef, small islands, or a sandbar, which is a long ridge of sand.

maglev train
A train that uses magnets called electromagnets to move at high speed. The magnets also lift the train so it floats slightly above the rail.

outback
A vast, desert-like area of Australia where very few people live.

pollution
Materials such as trash, chemicals, gases, and dust that can damage the air, water, or land. Cars and other vehicles that run on gasoline or diesel release polluting gases into the air from their exhaust.

rickshaw
A small vehicle that is often pulled by a person on foot or on a bicycle.

INDEX

A
animals 5, 12–13, 14–15

B
bicycles 8–9
buses 4, 6–7

C
canoes 10–11
cars 4, 21

D
dog sleds 13
donkeys 12

F
flying ambulances 18–19

G
getting to school 6–7, 8–9, 10–11, 20–21

H
horses 12

M
maglev trains 16
motorbikes 5, 8

P
planes 18–19

R
reindeer 4–5, 14–15
rickshaws 8–9

S
school buses 6–7, 8–9, 21
snowmobiles 14–15

T
trains 16–17

W
walking 20–21